To Joan and David,
for your reading
pleasure,
from Erika
December 2004

HELD
CAPTIVE

HELD CAPTIVE

Poems and Stories

by

Erika Zettl

Illustrations by Herbert Zettl

PAPERMILL CREEK PUBLISHING

Forest Knolls, California

Editor: Elizabeth von Radics

Designer: Gary Palmatier

Compositor: Ideas to Images

Printer: Prisma Graphic Corporation

Bindery: Roswell Bookbinding

Papermill Creek Publishing
P.O. Box 91
Forest Knolls, CA 94933

Printed in the United States of America

ISBN 0-9763014-0-7

First Printing

In memory of my mother

EMMA ELLA TRONICKE

Contents

Part II

In Bloom

Part III

Drifting Colors

Part IV

Winter Lights

PART I

Awakening

Haiku

1

From its small prison
the singing canary holds
its keeper captive

2

The branch, ripped off the
apple tree by winter storm,
begins to blossom

3

Garden snails hiding
in young lettuce—Silver trails
on leaves tell their path

4

A springtime downpour—
In muddy ditches dying
petals are dancing

5

In a small bottle
such costly perfume—Come, smell
my lilac blossoms!

6

Bushes, manicured,
planted in rows and patterns
wanting to grow free

THE VISIT

It's Sunday. On my way to see Ester at the convalescent hospital, I stop to check her garden. Her home stands silent now. Pine needles cushion the path to the entrance. Mailbox wide open, carport empty, curtains drawn. In contrast to the gloom, the garden bursts with color. Sparaxis, iris, rosemary, and wild onion compete for space. I gather shades of yellow, red, and blue into a tight bouquet, for Ester.

It's lunchtime at the hospital when I arrive. Patients in wheelchairs, fed by nurses, crowd hallways, dining rooms.

Ester is in her room with her tray of food untouched. She looks up, recognizes me. Joy in her face.

"These flowers are from your garden. Remember our ritual, when you invited me each spring to look at them?"

"Pretty flowers. Nice, nice." She smiles.

"Else sends best wishes. She called from Illinois last night." Ester looks puzzled, "Else? Else?"

"Your sister Else. Remember? She visited you last May."

Stroke impaired, her mind searches for Else. She looks so serious. She is trying so hard. Last year so alert, this year just fragments of memory. The bed next to her is empty.

"Ester, where is your roommate? She was asleep when I was here last week." We both look at the bed: new sheets, bedspread tucked in.

"I don't know."

"When did you see her last?"

"I don't remember."

There is no pillow on the bed. The nightstand bare, pictures gone. I inquire at the station. The head nurse tells me, "Ester's roommate died yesterday, at 3 a.m. It was to be expected."

I feel empty, return to the room. Ester looks at me, "What is it?"

"I don't know," I say.

From down the hall, a shriek, "Alice, Alice—help! Help!"

Nobody pays attention. Aides come and go. Ester pulls me close. Her hands are cold. Under her sweater, all bones. I hug her frame good-bye. Almost weightless, like a bird.

"I'll come again. Soon."

As I walk to the elevator, a faint smell of urine and antiseptic drifts from the rooms.

I try not to cry. Outside I stop under a flowering cherry. Draw fresh air into my lungs.

It's spring.

LAST RITE

The early morning rain
left the dead peach tree
diamond-studded.
A fragile shroud,
strings of tiny globes
clinging and trembling
in the sun.

A lively wren swoops down
and through its quiet touch
the diamonds drop like tears,
all but one.

Sharing the Path

Two glossy bodies
travel the same path—
one within the other
yet in opposite directions.
One stream, the other fish.
Stream presses its
abundant waters through
a narrow bed,
sea bound.
Its voices echo
through the valley.
Salmon slices its way
with dynamic strength
toward the source—
in silence.
Two pregnant shapes,
metallic flashes,
life-giving. Hastening
to meet their destinies.

Nature's Way

The weathered locust tree
outside my kitchen window
once more in festive robe.
White blossoms dangle
from thorned branches
like clusters of grapes
spreading their perfume.
Suddenly, as in a storm
approaching, vibrations, a roar,
noise of wings clapping.
Wild pigeons, dozens, land,
compete for blossoms.
Gray and purple shapes
flutter, balance, feast in haste.
A narrow band of white
around the nape,
yellow flashes of beaks and feet.
Branches tremble, twigs break,
flower petals, buds, dropping.
Then, as by command,
all birds fly off at once.

The locust tree remains,

depleted of its splendor.

Through lingering fragrance

a downy feather drifts to earth.

Paper Mill Creek

Winter brought rain.
Hills unload profuse waters,
swelling the creek.
New vigor, a lusty surge.
Blackberry vines reel in eddies;
boulders, tree branches, leave scars.
Soil loosens, muddies the stream.
Strong roots resist the force,
everything else must ride along to sea.
Thirsty, deer, raccoon, skunk
approach with hesitation.
Canyon amplifies the rushing roar.
Soon the creek's shouts
will be only a whisper.

ENCOUNTER

All morning I've been pulling weeds.
My dogs, tired of watching me
like supervisors, have retreated
into noontime shade.

On my way to the compost pile
I spot a furry head among the leaves.
Two pearly eyes are watching me.
I move closer, just a little.
"Is it a gopher? A baby squirrel?"
Body grayish brown,
handsome moustache,
but ears—like those
on Mickey Mouse hats
in Disneyland.

We remain motionless,
staring at each other.
How long, I can't remember.
Then he turns slowly,
disappears into the periwinkle,
dragging behind
his long, naked tail.

Spring Morning

During the early morning hours, when the sun begins to eat up valley mist, my garden beckons. I slip on my garden shoes and step outside. Crisp, moist air chills my skin. I pull my robe closer around my body. The sky hangs low, like a tie-dye in an array of grays and whites, allowing only glimpses into the expanse beyond.

Last night's rain purified the air. Slender branches of the cherry plums are bending low under the watery load, brushing against my face. Pearls drip off the leaves. The rain has glued the flower petals of the apple blossoms to each other. Those that escaped have piled up like silk confetti in the corners and crevasses of the garden steps.

The soil along the narrow path between the flowerbeds has turned to chocolate pudding. It holds my soles like suction cups, then releases them with smacking sounds. Columbine, lunaria, and forget-me-nots dominate the flower patch with a rich palette of blues and purples. Rosebuds are ready to open their pregnant shapes, revealing their color. A long-stemmed iris has lost its balance. Its rain-soaked head lies on the muddy ground. Invisible bugs have chewed lace designs into its sepals. I try to find a stake to help it stand again tall and proud.

Down by the fence, on vines that looked dead a few days ago, tiny leaves have exploded out of resin-coated winter capsules. A faint smell of skunk still lingers. I cannot see the creek that runs along the road, but I can hear its thunder as its swelled body pushes through the rocky bed. Before the rain, nothing but a muted trickle.

On my way back to the house, a breeze carries a rich taste of honey from the nearby lilac blossoms. My lungs open like sails to the fragrant air. All sleepiness is gone—I feel refreshed. My muddy shoes remain outside. I shake some drops of water from my hair and place a small bouquet of flowers in a vase on the breakfast table—a joyful "Good morning!" from my garden.

PART II

In Bloom

Haiku

———

7

Wet clouds float by, so
light—The watering can in
my hand, so heavy

8

The blazing dew drops
will be consumed by the sun
that brought them to life

9

Flaming hibiscus
opens its timeless splendor
for one day only

10

In the garden your
roses are blooming—On your
grave three dandelions

11

The waterlily
growing in murky water
stands in pristine white

12

When darkness steals all
color from my roses, their
fragrance comforts me

HILDA AND WALTER

Walter, already seated at the dinner table, starts to eat. "Hilda, bring a beer!"

"Please!" she admonishes him, wiping some scattered drops off the sparkling clean kitchen counter. "Here is your beer." She puts a glass and a bottle in front of Walter.

His fingers glide over the bottle. "This is too cold. It will ruin my voice."

"But it was in the fridge for only a few minutes."

"It's too cold. Bring me another one. —No, *no!* Not from the fridge. Get one from the box in the hallway."

Hilda joins Walter at the dinner table with the new bottle in her hand. "I hope someday I'll get it just right for you."

Walter is deep into the newspaper and his meal. "Did you read the review of our new performance of *Aida*?" he asks. "It's simply devastating. Our new conductor just doesn't seem to bring it together."

"Yes, I heard it from Bill. He's fed up with it, too."

"I've been on stage now for forty-five years—did you hear me, Hilda?—forty-five years! And I've never seen it that bad."

"Well, times change."

"What do you mean, 'times change'? *Aida* is *Aida*. A classic!"

"Maybe you've changed."

"Me? No chance. I never change."

"But you did, when you moved from soloist to singing in the chorus."

"Ah, that's different. It would have ruined my health if I hadn't. You know, too much stress. —Why do you laugh, Hilda?"

"Oh, it's not about your health. I just remember the conductor telling you at that time: 'Keep in mind that from now on it is no longer Walter singing *with* the chorus but Walter singing *in* the chorus.'"

"Why are you always so mean to me, Hilda? All my colleagues tell me that I am doing fine. They think I have excellent stage presence and still a strong voice. We all get along great." Walter dives into the paper again while sipping his new beer.

Hilda tells him, "I saw my doctor today. He thinks my blood pressure is still too high. He recommends that I reduce the stress I'm under."

"What stress?" says Walter.

"Well, just stress, like right now."

"I think you have it pretty easy. Nice home, good part-time job, and *me,* your loving husband." Walter grabs Hilda's arm, expands his chest, and sings fortissimo in his voluminous baritone voice the famous aria from Mozart's *Don Giovanni:* "Give me your hand, my love, and I'll guide you to my castle." He raises his right hand and conducts the rest of the solo with his knife.

Hilda withdraws her arm. "That's not it. I miss some—"

"Miss what? Don't you like Mozart? *Wolfgang Amadeus Mozart.* I don't see anything missing in your life. I just bought the new couch you wanted."

"It's just that I feel …"

"Just take the blood-pressure pills your doctor prescribed and you'll feel OK. Speaking of feelings, how do you feel about Fred leaving us? He's lucky, I guess. Got a job in London."

"Good for him."

"I wonder whether they'll look for his replacement in the chorus. With all the funding cuts."

"Walter, my doctor thinks that I should take a vacation."

"I think I saw something about the budget cuts in this paper. Where is it now? *Hmm,* I can't find it. There is so much other stuff in this paper. You can't find anything important in this crummy paper anymore."

"The doctor thinks I should go on a vacation. By myself."

"Don't you think Fred is lucky? He found another job right away. Lucky. Eh, what did you say? Going on vacation by yourself? Ah, you don't want to go by yourself, do you? Give me some more noodles. Good, they're hot."

"You want another beer?"

"Yes, but not too cold." With a sure hand Walter pours the not-too-cold beer into his glass and watches the froth rise to a 1½-inch head. "Perfect! You know, Hilda, they told me that I should consider retirement. For next fall, perhaps. I really wouldn't know what I'd do with all this free time, away from the stage—from art, from culture."

Hilda twists her paper napkin into a tight ball, forcing herself to listen to him.

"After forty-five years of my life on stage, always surrounded by music, beautiful music—I'd feel cut off from everything— from my dear colleagues." He pauses, turns to Hilda, and sings in

Puccini's tragic voice of Rodolfo: "What shall I do? Oh, my beloved Hilda, what shall I do?"

Hilda rises from her chair, the paper ball clutched in her fist. "Perhaps you should apply as a doorman at the opera when you retire. Then you can see your good friends every day."

A Summer Day in West Marin

A cloudless sky
spans sun-parched land.
Air heavy with a smell of clay.
A hard-baked road,
crusty and cracked, meanders
alongside velvet knolls
like camel humps
in flickering heat.
Golden grasses line the path,
pointing up bristly heads.
Among dry weeds
on leafless, spindly twigs
bloom little yellow stars
as if by some mistake.
Behind ramshackle fences
cows crowd into midday shade
under two lonely oaks.
A red-tailed hawk floats
on cushions of warm air.

Distant, speeding cars,
a chain saw's biting sound,
vibrations from a heavy truck.
The ripe seeds shudder.

Monarchs

As fiery clouds of orange
against the summer sky
monarchs did undulate, circle.
Exalted I watched them fly.

Their Mexican roosts depleted,
where forests did abound
the butterflies searched for shelter—
found death on barren ground.

In northern groves their brothers
surprised by frost and rain,
frozen in grapelike clusters
their huddled pupas remain.

Today, to my flower garden
a lone survivor came back,
reminding me with his colors
that orange is rimmed with black.

THE MORNING GLORY

A California town.
Afternoon heat
weighs on the streets.
Asphalt soft as dough.
A young couple hastens
to a nearby restaurant.
He halts. A vacant lot
arrests his view.
Hundreds of morning glories,
blue and purple, blooming
on arid ground,
blanket debris and dust.
He bends down, picks
one flower, holds the velvet
chalice close to his face.
Joy in his eyes.
She turns in anger,
"Don't take that. I don't like it.
It brings bad luck."
He drops the flower;
they walk on in silence.
The morning glory left to die.

Two years later, the man,
divorced, visits the lot.
Bulldozers, like giant bugs,
digging for new construction.

AQUA VITAE

I walk cocooned in my own skin,
a shield against the blistering heat
on this rain-hungry earth.
A scorching path, my toes curl up,
swimming pool beckons.
I dive into the mirrored image
of sky, oak trees, petunia blossoms.
Fragmented by my strokes,
patches of blue, green, red
drift apart, collide, realign.
Strings of white, like silken threads,
unravel, float along my body,
then dissolve.
Eyes almost blinded, turn inward.
All sense of time is lost.
Stress flows out;
my energy expands.
A rhythm from within comes
forth and takes control.

As I return to air and soil,
emerging from my wet embrace,
the furrow on the water's
wrinkled face narrows
and turns to glass.

WILDFIRE

Abandoned by campers,
sheltered by trees,
a smoldering fire
sleeps like a kitten.
Whipped by gusts,
it wakes in anger, hisses.
Tame friend turns savage.
A fiery beast rises, stretches
its mighty body, roars.
Gleaming eyes sparkle.
With ferocious speed,
wild fury, leaps ahead,
suddenly changing direction.
Mane flaming, lashes the air.
Stalking, it pauses,
then pounces at new prey,
licks it with red hot tongue,
devours it. Insatiable hunger.
The hunting ground
expands with rapid pace.
Death lines its path,
color melts to gray.

Men, in awe, watching
the demon approach,
muster all forces—
Days of fierce battle.
At last the brute, surrounded
and subdued, retreats,
hides among cinders.
Men, vigilant, stay on guard.
Red eyes still glow at night,
get weaker, dimmer, paler.
Dying breath poisons the air.
There is no sky.
The sun seems lost—
A wasteland fills the space.
Black shapes, trunks without limbs,
ribbons of smoke.
Next spring, amidst the ashes,
lupines will bloom.

Part III

Drifting Colors

Haiku

13

Juicy blackberries
sweet taste on my tongue,
scratches on my hands

14

Our old vizsla lies
stretched out before her igloo—
The cat sleeps inside

15

Three shiny pebbles
lifted from the crystal creek—
In my hand, dull stones

16

The Golden Gate Bridge
shrouded in ocean-gray fog
spans into nowhere

17

In my garden, our
dog digs up the tulip bulbs
that I just planted

18

The World Trade Towers
brought down by terrorist act—
In nothing rests all

Tahoe Autumn Quintet

The Town

Main street parades vacancy signs.
A sudden gust of wind plays tetherball
with a tossed paper cup
across an empty parking lot.
Firewood stacked against houses.
Jack-o-lanterns grin from thresholds.
The homeless, more prominent now,
in haste looking for shelter.

The Mountains

Mountain peaks, like canines,
bite into the sky. Rugged detail,
edged by autumn light,
brought close. One can almost
touch the weathered rock.
Frayed patches of snow cling
like wet tissue in crevasses.
Bare slopes waiting for winter.

The Lake

A platinum disc reflects the scene
upside down. Five migrant geese
land, ruffle their shadow on the gloss.
Waves lapping over the beach,

wipe out imprints of bare feet—
soon to be replaced by patterns
of profiled boots, big dogs' paws.
Tufts of grass, sun-bleached,
wave and bend like strands of silken hair.
Frost will render them brittle.

The Woods

In wooded groves silence can be heard.
Pine scent mixes with a whisper of winter.
Sun rays slant through branches,
cast lacework shadows over boulders.
Pine cones collect like eggs
in nests around the granite.
Ground squirrel stuffs its cheeks
with scraps of littered paper,
then hurries underground.

The Meadows

In Alpine meadows
between lake and woods
color and texture join.
Light fawn, sorrel, rust, sienna
appear in smooth and bristly.
Branches snap, seeds scatter.
Summer has been long.
A last rich offering.

SUMMER'S LAST ROSE

In my garden
untouched by early frost,
a solitary rose.

Fragile as eggshell porcelain.
The color of the harvest moon,
its half-open, silken robe
holds secrets, promises.

Captivated by its beauty
I place the fragrant flower
in your caring hands.
Our fingers touch—
a surge of joy.

A Thousand Suns

By the roadside,
aspens.
Rows of golden columns
like the pillars of
Mayan temples.
Each holds
a thousand little suns
on fragile threads.
The mood
of parting lovers
trying to hold on.
The glow fades
to dimmer shades
of longer darkness.
White stars will soon
renew the wonder.

THE WEEPING WILLOW

You have stood here
longer than I remember.
A single tree surrounded
by a barren yard.

A twisted shape,
trunk split, concealed
by drooping branches, their
ribbons swaying in the wind.

Crown lush, sheltering
secret nooks, resonant with
children's laughter, bird calls,
the silences of dreamers.

You, who survived
so many storms and winters,
surrendered to a silent
breeze, last night.

I found you dying
with limbs broken,
your shadow buried
under your weeping head.

November Day

Gray morning veils have lifted.
I see the world grow wide.
Fir trees, ignored by frost,
watch as their neighbors die.
Apple trees still hold
a few golden leaves,
while cherry plums, denuded,
wear crimson skirts
around their base.
A cold sun rises.
Potted geraniums
held in tight bouquets
let autumn shadows
creep up their stems.

I feel a wintry chill.
A notice in my hand
tells me my father died.
I, among fir trees,
stay behind.

GRANDMA'S PICTURE

Fragments of an old photograph lie scattered on my desk and on the floor. Sadness slows my movements. I try to piece the scraps together, let Grandma's faded image take form like in a jigsaw puzzle: Here is part of her lively face, her amber eyes—she used to watch me from her balcony when I hiked up the steep hill from the railroad station for a visit. Her hair—torn off. She always wore it piled up high, turned into a twist, secured by giant pins. She dyed it with a homemade extract of green walnut shells, her secret. I often wondered why Grandma never turned gray and remained fifty-six forever. Her small nose—only a trace of it left—delighted in the fragrances of lilac-scented soap, blooming violets by the creek, and dried bouquets wedged among petticoats and handkerchiefs in her messy chest of drawers. Sniffing and smelling were our rituals. Yet her keen sense of smell seemed unaware of overdue cheeses, or apples rotting in her pantry.

I can find only a small fragment of her mouth, bracketed by two impish dimples, that reinforced her smile. Her mouth, her tongue, were in constant motion: talking to neighbors, friends, even strangers. Guests were always welcome in her modest house; the white tablecloth with the border of roses, fresh-cut flowers in a vase, crunchy bread from the bakery, and a glass of wine, already waiting. When home alone, she sang. At first with a full voice, later with a raspy sound; but still, she sang!

Her willowy body, nestled in an overstuffed armchair, is distorted by the crumpled piece of paper. Half white—that was her blouse, half black—her full skirt, covering the buckled shoes. I can't find her hands. But, shown folded as in prayer, they weren't really hers anyway, but merely part of the photographer's desired pose. In fact, her hands were always busy, collecting various herbs for teas, starting plants from cuttings, or steering her Model A Ford with skill along the narrow streets. Yet these hands would never sew or mend. Glue worked just fine for her when patching up holes in fabric. Thread and needles were left to tailors and seamstresses.

On her buffet a shrine of family pictures. "Someday, when I die," she would tell me many times, "I want you to have my picture. This one in the copper frame." Many years later, this picture spoke to me from my own desk.

The antique copper frame, hand-wrought with elaborate flowers, made the photograph look dignified. The burglars took the frame, but left the picture ripped to shreds. So securely mounted into its frame, was it unwilling to let go of its support? There are just too many pieces missing to reconstruct the photo. Angry and sad, I sweep the fragments off my desk and toss them into the fireplace, then watch flames once more consume Grandma's remnants. My eyes turn inward, to where her picture will remain forever, even without a frame.

PART IV

Winter Lights

HAIKU

19

The sun leaves my world
taking along all color—
The moon paints it white

20

The autumn leaves gone—
Frozen branches cradle new
buds waiting for spring

21

Nothing but thick fog
on my familiar road home—
I am feeling lost

22

On fresh fallen snow
small footprints stitch a pattern—
A lone feather drifts

23

White cloak of winter
covering the town's graveyard
makes all look equal

24

My snowman with his
carrot nose has a warm smile—
Oh, my cold fingers!

First Winter Rain

The sun has burnt the land.
Gold turned to brown.
One Indian summer day
I drive to town
under an azure sky,
a vaultlike canopy
over the valley.
Mirages dissolve
as I approach.

Suddenly, a pregnant
cloud rips the canvas,
bursts under its own weight,
empties all pockets.
Earth's parched mouth
opens wide,
water swells her body.
Sheets of rain
slapping against my doors.
Oil puddles, devils,
eye with rainbow iris
at my wheels—
are pepper-sprayed

by passing cars
with muddy water.
My windshield wipers click
in two-four measure;
I hum along
a long-forgotten tune.

In town, rain gutters
hammer a metallic beat.
Fountains spouting
over sidewalks
choke drains with leaves
and scraps of paper.
Drops snake
down my brow,
garments, limp rags,
cool my frame.
As the heat's
tight embrace loosens,
moisture nourishes my fabric.
I toss my worries
in the drain, watching
them swirl away.
My lungs, like parachutes,
open to dust-free air.
Umbrellaless, I tiptoe
to the supermarket.

Along the road
on my way home,
two little boys
in rubber boots hop
into muddy puddles,
laughing, splashing—
I feel like joining them.

CANDLELIGHT

Candles shine everywhere—
on altars, tables, trees, in windows,
add thoughtfulness to old traditions,
solemnity to rituals.

Candles of different color,
scent, shape, size
do not discriminate
between cathedral, temple,
mosque, or shrine.
Their radiance is equal.

Candles replenish hearts
with festive glow.
Their mellow light dispels
the shadows of the soul,
bridles the force
of human frenzy.

Captured by the stillness
of the moment,
eyes shine, hands reach out.
Each candle holds
a seed of hope.

JACK'S PLACE

Jack's house next door stands silent now.
Tall grasses take command of yard and orchard,
half-buried flower pots, all sizes,
no longer tended by his hands.
Driveway dusty, rutted
by many workbound wheels;
two rusty cars next to the hulk of a garage.
Main gate, wide open, latchless.

Deer, last year's intruders—this year's
residents—move undisturbed on paths
that Jack walked every day:
at first with energetic strides,
later with cane, then crutches.
He often came to chat across the fence.
Each time a different story.
One day his brittle bones
shattered in a fall.

Brown leaves hide
fragments of china, broken bottles.
Indifferent to Jack's years of toil and effort,
nature claims back what once was hers.
Skeleton frames of garden lounges
under aged oak trees, quiet reminders.

AYALA

Your mother calls, telling me, "Ayala died this morning of lung infection." Unbelievable pain. My throat feels tight. "I'll come right over," I say.

Morning fog crawls over the ridge. Along the roadside bare trees, brown weeds under the low, winter sky.

Your mother greets me, her face ashen, eyes empty. Alone, she mourns the loss her husband with a recent stroke no longer comprehends. I bring azaleas, bright red, her favorite color, a contrast to the desolation of the room. A grateful nod, a shine in her eyes.

Quietly, we sit down, with your framed portraits already lined up on the table. A small worn photo album holds baby pictures of you in Jerusalem, your birthplace.

When I first met you, you were a schoolgirl, had mastered English in just half a year. Your light brown hair in long, thick braids. Blue eyes, alert, friendly.

Your mother's place is silent now. As I unpack a lunch, the paper plates seem loud. Next to our table, a sliding glass door opens to the patio and garden. Unexpected, a deer approaches from the bushes, halts by the door, statuelike. Startled by the strange visitor, your mother asks, "Is it a female?"

"Yes, it is," I say.

She nods in thought. Ayala, we remember your life like a batik: colorful, layered, dark over bright. You were an only child, a successful student, a college graduate. Alcohol abuse ended your promising career. You moved to Colorado. Recovery. Beginning of a new life.

As we start eating our whole-wheat sandwiches, the doe remains, watching us, unafraid. In subdued voices we recall your last visit. A trip to the beach; our bare feet pressing into wet sand. Cool ocean breezes ballooning our skirts. We felt like flying. In the evening a festive dinner, saying good-bye. Then your illness. Your mother buries her face in her hands.

When she looks up she sees the deer still standing outside, motionless. We watch in silence as it turns slowly and disappears.

Gazing into an empty yard, I hear your mother's pleading voice, "Ayala, is this a sign from you for me?" There is no answer. Breaking the silence she turns to me and says, "Her Hebrew name 'Ayala' means 'female deer.'"

Departure

I still remember the main
railroad terminal downtown.
A massive metal frame,
blackened by soot.
The vaulted roof spanned in front
by yellowed windows
filtering beams of light.
Between high, raised platforms,
steam locomotives puffing,
rolling to a screeching halt,
others snorting in their stalls.
Air thick with steam and smoke.
Passengers swarming in all directions,
clutching their cardboard tickets
with the small punched hole,
stopping at posted schedules
for a last-minute confirmation
of arrival or departure time.
Then pressing to the proper platform
along rows of newsstands,
flower kiosks, shoeshine benches.
Shouts of vendors, offering
cigarettes, hotdogs, fruit.
Porters pushing rumbling carts.

Oblivious to all this bustling,
three street-wise sparrows
darting down, hopping deftly
to find some morsel on the ground.
The piercing sound of a shrill whistle,
the train conductor's raised round disc.
Some frantic pushing, scrambling.
Laughter and tears.
A quick embrace, a daring jump
onto the footboards of the train.
All doors slam shut,
the wheels grind into motion.
Traffic signals click,
grainy ash clouds the view.
Oil-spotted railroad ties,
shiny rails await a new arrival.
The giant clock ticks on.

SHADOW

One day he stood outside
my kitchen door,
reminding me of Halloween.
Head, legs, tail black,
body with shades of brown.
Fur matted, bones protruding
from a skinny frame,
eyes yellow, shining like stars.
He came for months
at dinnertime.
Shy at first, later
allowing me to pet him
while he ate.
At dark he vanished
in the empty lot next door.
I called him Shadow.

"There is a dead cat
in the street by our gate,"
my husband said,
coming home from work.
"Looks like Shadow.
Must have been hit by a car."

I find a carcass lying
on its side, stiff,
mouth bloody.
Tears dropping on
the cat's black fur,
I hear a voice,
as from afar, say,
"We'll have to bury him."

At dinnertime,
a black shape waits
outside my kitchen door.
I'm startled.
Two yellow eyes beg
for food, "Meow, meow."
It's Shadow.

HAIKU

25

His love has left him—
Her dog returned, sits waiting
at the open gate

26

Our jet flying west
upsetting my rhythm of time—
The sun floats along

27

The graceful figure
of an African woman
carved in ivory

28

I am too busy
to rest in my new easy chair—
The cat owns it now

29

Nobody will sit
on your needlepoint pillow—
Those tiny stitches

30

In timeless orbits
the earth travels undisturbed
by man's hasty pace

A Candle for My Mother

Quiet cathedral.
I light a candle
for my mother.
Its flame joins others
already burning.
Unknown mourners.
I'm not alone
in my grief.